Chrysalis in the Desert

Also by Wendy Saloman:

Syllables and Leaves

WENDY SALOMAN

Chrysalis in the Desert

Shearsman Books
Exeter

First published in the United Kingdom in 2009 by
Shearsman Books Ltd
58 Velwell Road
Exeter EX4 4LD

www.shearsman.com

ISBN 978-1-84861-036-1

First edition

Copyright © Wendy Saloman, 2009.

The right of Wendy Saloman to be identified as the author of this work has been asserted by her in accordance with the Copyrights, Designs and Patents Act of 1988. All rights reserved.

Acknowledgements:
Acknowledgment and thanks are due to *Poetry Salzburg Review* in which 'Rivers and Revenants' and 'Cassandra' were first published.

Cover image:
'Wounded Angel' (1967) by Cecil Collins (1908–1989),
copyright © Tate, London 2009.
Photograph by Clive Hicks.

In memory of my parents

Contents

Of Beginnings	9
Rivers and Revenants	10
And where / In the Faustian flow of the river	18
Cassandra	19
Once into Nothing	24
In Strange October Light	26
Quarrying the Mind	27
Resurrection of Crocuses	28
August Epiphany	34
Crowned by Death	36
Engraved on Sky	37
Then Hearing You	38
How Distant You Were	39
And Under the Sun	40
Chrysalis in the Desert	41
Here Over the Midnight Sea	65
Light-Speech	66
Gorse-Light	71
Knowing-Well of Silence	74
She Sings This Perfect City	77
Roman Hour	78
Faustina	81
Toward the Midnight	82
Yesterday's Domain	86
Fragments	90

Of Beginnings—

Words floating through white spaces of time

descending— to the place where fear hides

ash-words from which the phoenix may rise

words fished from waters—

rough as those that rocked the Ark

words binding sea and sky with ephemeral promises

words shaming crimes— defending the violated

words seeking healing of an angel

rose-coloured words offered to the dead

marmoreal words hewn by love

words weathered on stone

words metamorphosing on the winds

words of exile riding on nostalgia

weightless words shining as the chrysalis in the desert

words thrown to stars questioning God and the universe:

and where do they come from, these words

if not from the silence before a poem is born.

Rivers and Revenants

"only two nightingales didn't know Yiddish"
                              Vytautas Bložė

1

Let me dig into a hush of this riverland
fill lacuna
with noise of the past
—speak of the dwelling-up names

amid spruce and pine
let birdsong be testament

and there in the dust
—where memory of Vytautas
offering migrants a measure of a land
long ago passed
over water gilded by autumn
let me enter a language of gods
—hear purity of sound
in libations to Žemyna
and in sanctification by a *chazan* of the One:

let skies, charged
by fragments of myths
—by script of wild geese
over fields and marshes
recollect a winter light
its dark intelligence
glowing between knots of otherness
between word and act
between amen and shadow.

2

—And slowly flows the Dabikinė
taking history
to mock eternity of the sea—
changing winds
blow music of tufted seeds across it
still flies the crane
still hovers a thrush nightingale

—with promises of the earth
it winds
through meadow, birch wood
where once there was a farmstead
where once there was the word— Jew

at the water's edge I imagine you
hearing the word— your name in the word
and the psalms echoing through grasses

—summering-out it flows
as if in remembrance
of drifting scents of sabbaths
freshly baked challah, lit candles, breath of kiddush
while sistering trees— in effulgence
reflect to infinity—

what if there had been— no budding May Laws
no flower of poverty
no journey from east to west?

yes— the river would go on
to leaf-song, hymn of reeds, evening shadows of hatreds

and we— in time
between pine trees you praised
and the silence of old gods you refuted
would belong in a grief-flow of the murdered.

3

—There was otherness
there was snow
there was the ice-flow down-river
and thousandfold
there were pine-needles
bitten into
by insult in the air—
but here
where field empties into field
and earth smells of nostalgia
festive laughter
from Purim to Chanukah
once mingled
with joy of Kovno's myths—
a burden of separateness
carried weightless by the air
while each blade of grass
vulnerable in the wind
hummed upward
to the sanctity of the Unnameable.

4

Under which constellation
did you speak your last to the river you loved—
in what dark solace
did the lamp of your name glimmer?
In field and forest—
where hawk hunts the song of thrush
you hid a Jew's sorrow
in stone, pine-needles, heartwood of oak
—of boyhood
you hid memories in the reeds at night
but the cold of a dawn held clarity
—in both hands
you took light from your dream of Elijah
to journey to new river, new land.

And when the ash of Avaslan
gathered upward with dust
and with breath of a stork forced from its nest
some said a star looked on
—held a dialogue with the earth.

5

To address the river, as you did
seek exchange—
a moment of history for a currency of myth
here where autumn looks to eternity

to speak out amid grasses
of absence as presence—
a path untrodden for years by foot of a Litvak

to hear in the voices of forests
echoes of Cain
and all those conspiracies
still interrogated by the moon

to walk in remembrance of words forgotten

is to reclaim the dead, silences, leaf-fall—
the angel of the plough— unwinged by poverty

is to rename the light—
resonant once with the letters of your God.

6

Quiet the slow flow, the dark angel
the invisible letters of *thou shalt not kill*
quiet all scars on the roughland of history—
but we, the listening ones
recognise the pulse of a psalm
fragment of prayer, quiver of pines
—an hour of terror looking backward to God

with our hearing-souls
we take from earth's memory
dislocated song—
throat-up pure syllables
—voice across the river an offering to the massacred.

7

Winged on a ray of light
over a thread of rained-on river
over a script of copper leaf
a crow brings speech back from the dead
—it tells of a dream of fig and vine
and clod of earth— the homecoming
—of a butterfly hovering
over a word, a rose, a glow
over an archaic promise
for a land burnished over by myth.

8

Word— our word
grown on an angel's wing

(and Jacob humbled and arrogant
after his midnight struggle).

Once prince amid words.
Once lamented by the prophets.

Then came snow over the word
and over centuries of footsteps—
and o the whiteness of piety
and song of yearning covering the earth.

The rose in the word
the yes and the no—
the will and the willed-for

flowering—
dividing—
thorns dispossessing
where once petals were dispossessed.

Word— and a bee
taking from a wound of the word
—bittering . . .

9

Shall I beneath this cinnamon sky
near to dusk
give ear to the enigma of ancestral roots
here by the river
where the past in its quiet lies inert:
shall I assume the wind haunts reeds
while waiting
for an instrument of remembrance:
and shall I walk
through leafage of years
commit my voice
with chirruping birds
to inexhaustible song
and ephemeral ownership—
for we are
are we not
guests on this earth
tuned by threads of light
on a moment of narrative?

10

Imagine, heavenward
praise for an angel wrestling with a river god
—praise of the forests
and summer's scent
of strawberries in the undergrowth
rising to morning cumulus:
—imagine birds in full throat
chorusing
above cadences of Yiddish . . .
—a dance, an orchard
a fiddler praising a bride with music
as if she were the Shulammite:
imagine coming to market
a Jew— with fruits of the earth
praise blossoming into a poem
casting seeds
numerous as the dead:
imagine breath of faith
dazzling
when barks of yellowing birches
are utterance of dusk:
—then speak of memory
grown over by burdock
—murmurings of the Talmud
travelling graveward— here
in a landscape of rivers and revenants.

AND WHERE
IN THE FAUSTIAN FLOW OF THE RIVER

In memory of E.G.S.

And where
in the Faustian flow of the river
a bird passes through cloud
imaged on water
there is also that going-toward
that hinterland of quiet

that re-entering of life into listening

that waiting for the dead
their voices rooted
in cracks of earth's memory
stammering upward— to claim air

and there
when you reached over
touched me with words
laminated by war
I heard thread-through with light
a young man's heart-beat
on the scales of justice
with a poet's quest for gravity and grace

all the purity of Beatrice
of Laura
transferred to daughter of a river god
—Lady of the Laurel
yours, ever unobtainable
yours, ever dream-bright.

Cassandra

*"—to lift to my lips the hand
of one who killed my son."*
                    The Iliad

. . . And they wept tears of light
and she wept with them
for in their hands there was grace

but then in a shadow of the dream
fear filled her throat— spewed-out
and vowels reverberated
through shell, seakale, granite—

Apollo whipped up the wind
the sea ravaged her voice
taking it everywhere and nowhere.

It was the nightbird who mimicked
the ironies of war—
it was the creature risen from the sands
who shouted of pity.

*

Dead, Cassandra, dead, yet present here
running across the shore
her voice rising to meet the sea—
each word dazzling the intelligence of fish
swimming southward to the future—

The moment passes, estranged she turns
her body wrapped by the wind's stark music
her face washed-over with pain.

Winged above fragments of time
the gulls inherit her cries.

*

Now her voice in the dark shout of leaves
blasphemes against the lord of madness—
he who plays with light.

The season falters on.
The south wind vies with the north.
Obeisant, the grass endures.

And the trees turn their eyes heavenward.

Glitter on glitter, a coinage
of speech unblest
continues to violate tomorrows.

*

—We listen for her at dusk
when the thrush returns to the oak
and the sky is protective of its secrets.

Sometimes we hear syllables rise from her throat
as if the god had already broken them—

sometimes they sing out
autumnal vibrations
unchanged on an unchanging down-path.

This girl of dream and darkness enters us.
The dead also make music from the violence of light.

★

And look, her voice cries
how the fleeing leave with their footprints
for those who will follow
a midnight light of terror—

the sky takes up all grief.

Look how birds on the gravity of branches
sing of the fictions of ancestral rivers
and of the disinterred anger of the dead—

the roots of trees mourn for the blood.

Soon no one will know accuser from accused
nor the truth of the wasteland from speech on the wind.

Look how dust rises to the hovering amen.

Unwinged, the angel of history weeps.

*

Then carried on the waves
the awakening—

her voice lifts past the unsurprised shore
past thorn-bush and gorse
and moss-grown ears of stone—
past a nexus of shadows
and a bird shedding light on the lawn—

past the ilex trees
their leaves sheltering uneasy quiet
in a dawn constellation of rain—

her breath turns
entering our room, budding all-whiteness
here— in the still-land of listening.

*

Gilded, somewhere
a cry of self-mockery
issues from the throat of a gull

through thin air
the sound is dispersed

and broken echoes journey on light
to the interstices of matter.

Still she walks the shore
seeking affirmation in shells
and in the waves
returning to her voices of the dead.

*

—And above, diminishing
a hymn of stars
below, a warmonger's prelude.

The dead warn of flowering insanity
waves echo the dark side of the moon
gulls gyrate
carriers of uncertainty
for old wounds do not put down armouries
to seek a needle in ownerless desert.

Godlit, her voice shatters
falls where particles of sound are soon forgotten.

Ready to dance
the Furies fill the universe with music.

*

The city creeps into fog—
a fugitive of its own furtive violence.

Negated, the syllables of her anger freeze.

Will the smell of this twilight
with its stagnant water
tangle of trees
and columns of stone rising to nowhere
sharpen the nostrils already breathing in fear?

Will someone chisel the silence
release the fire, believe her?

*

*May summer bear witness to your voice
and seeds of oak and ash
these your trees, disseminate it.*

*May stone speak out
when the sea loses impetus—
when gulls let go their cries
before the hand of each murderous act.*

*May the god— living and dying in you
climb his own light.*

Once Into Nothing

Once into nothing
did the gods fall
then into darkness
fell the Yes and the No—
now as autumn reddens
across the lake
and the sun empties
its ferocious heat
blackbirds are silent
sparrows not to be seen—
hovering amid berries
a white-winged butterfly
is deceived.
Through ministering trees
breath of humankind
mingles with root-cries
with decomposing petals
of valedictory blood-flowers:
like a radiant knife
the word Why penetrates the air.

In Strange October Light

"... for a bird of the air shall carry the voice."
                    Ecclesiastes, X.20

In strange October light they felled the rowan
the dying one
in which yesterday's grief had nested.
Ever transient— ever hope-carriers
scarlet berries lay in the street
like skeletal promises.
Winging-over— a blackbird— sun-ravaged
bore testimony
for all tomorrow's half-spoken sorrows.

Quarrying the Mind

Quarrying the mind—
the philosopher's stone
ungraspable:
but dwelling there
earth's guardian
the erect pine
takes gold from its root
and reaches-up
to the drama in the sky
with equilibrium.

Resurrection of Crocuses

February's frost— a wintering-through
a resurrection of crocuses
a crow preening on the grass.
I walk a path to the dark edge of the earth
and the past follows me.
Then with the tongue of a quiet orient
your words beckon me toward light.
I stumble into your tenderness.

*

March, hyacinth days—
tears for the fallen youth
from whom Apollo took back light.
We have risked love for pride
sought in the undergrowth of ourselves
nothing more than a loss of image.

*

The I penetrates
strips the image of itself naked—
a word quivers
like a butterfly unsure of the dawn—
then love returns
to its place in the universe.

*

Dawn lifts its yellow arm
reveals to us
a small measure of the past.
But it is now, you say
now that is the fire
in the throat of the bird—
we have no equal beauty
to ameliorate the wound
we see reflected in the light.

*

Up-dwelling
the language of the eye—
crows
lording the river's edge
as if waiting for eternity—
sun-washed arms of silver birches
blessing a larkspur sky
while light across mud
dances to salutatory grasses. . .
But when
the eye looks at the I
and a down-dwelling truth
speaks to another—
there
in the tear
—the image breaks.

*

. . . Being here
summering in the arms of hills
hearing wind direct clouds
chant of light and shade
birdsong prayerlike
a peacock sounding strange harmonies
—desire and the tremor of leaves
mingling with a narrative of the river
with remembrance of stone
. . . being with you
walking through marlpools
as if they were left-over dreams
or poems not yet written
smelling the hawthorn and briar-rose
imagining us growing purewards
dwelling here in a moment
—belonging.

*

Now to a field of flux
we surrender
letting go all seeds of fear
pulsing in the fire of our blood—

how the wind
takes them through grasses
how wet earth receives them
as it does fearlessness of the dead

forward we cry our way
holding in both hands a sign of love
radiant whiteness
radiant hopefulness—
but on the other side of the path
nature's violence continues—

Into open sky another scream rises . . .

★

Ascend, you say
to where summer flowers
and all things sing all-bright.
No, I reply
we must descend
let the music begin
where the roots of our frailty
glow by grace—
then earth will resound
with all-dazzling Amen.

★

Whiteness was the dream
white the sea, the shore
white the creature on the rock
perched— judging us.
White the violent words we'd used

there washed-up—
shimmering, metamorphosed.
And in our hands— the offering
an all-white flower budded-out.
Silence on the wind the blessing.

*

Listen, I am here on the coast of our love
gathering all the unspoken—
January glows
as if it were a newly healed hand
opening to twitterings of a bird—

Listen, I am here
stringing together gentlenesses of years
to make from time a bracelet
to wear until death
and bequeath to children—

Beneath the earth
crocuses drink from our silences
whilst the tree— the one I name— Trust
takes our breath and sings— heavenward.

Listen—
before cloud diminishes us.

*

And over roughing winter water
flies the bird of time
cautiously
a boat moves into the future—

day climbs down
memories recede
trees become visible only to night—

by some miracle of crocus-light
in your eyes, in mine
we exchange silences
and listen for that secret
unravelling in the gull's throat
sounding along the river
beyond fear
beyond death . . .

August Epiphany

This blackbird on a breath of joy
taking its chance in the universe

this threshold of quiet in the garden . . .

we linger among essence of marigolds
wait for the moon to rise in our blood
say— here is memory, here the forgetting

this place where light enters sadness
and weight of transgression
each against other
dissolves in a handful of air

this Orphic wind with dry taste of August
touching our skin, exciting us
—into cumulus
we read the passage of love

—this dialogue opening-out
between nature and myth

thistledown-drift seeking stillness of earth
as if carrying pure thought—

an embrace of butterflies
choreographed by fate
stirring-up a currency of dust . . .

this summering we name ours
with words grown out of fire
like wild-eyed poppies and sun-drenched scabias

this speech of time and space
bringing us close to that sign of Thanatos
shining— there in the undergrowth

this shadow toward which the bird flies.

Crowned by Death

Crowned by death— your last tear
written on Cassiel's lake.
With hand grown like your hand
I cast a net
to catch reflection of mother and daughter.
But there on the shore
into its own shadow
falls the unspoken
forever driftwood, forever question.

Engraved on Sky

Engraved on sky—enduring—waves, whiteness
as if strands of your hair
had left the purity of death to move over the earth
. . . but you loved life with fire
tongued it with tenacity of forebears
and here in the blood— a memory bird
sings out in russet-tones
a melody prescribed for all mourners.
Of the secrets— those buried with you
it trills of a posthumous rose
rooted in a twilight of fear
and in the knot of your Hebraicness.

Then Hearing You

—Then hearing you
when time melts at midnight
into memory's rose-dust

hearing how you turned
from dreams of youth

turned from the place
where the wind blows the past
through quiet self-forgiving

turned from the dark
even when it cradled all the cold
and all forgetting
—the nuptials
breaking of the glass
mazeltov's
rising with praise of God:

imagining you
amid creases of white linen
surrendering to an act of love
as if this were hearing
the first prelude— to my life

—then hearing you
at midnight's edge
return to the longed-for
fullness of being on this earth

hearing you

hearing music
in an ever-open anti-room of death.

How Distant You Were

How distant you were
but there, in your otherness

each morning holding the ivory book
intoning prayer
quiet as a sun
rising from Abraham's blood

on your breath
the colour of faith
was that of a nurtured garden.

How distant you were
but there, in the Kaddish
grey on my lips.

And Under the Sun

"And the sun is a stain of your innocent blood."
                    Chaim Nachman Bialik

And under the sun— in an instant
the uniqueness of each of their beings
ceased—

on dust-dazzled streets
smelling of summer
just when there was a going-toward
a quiet movement of hope
their bodies entered the land
of Nothingness—

mourners wept tears hard as obsidian
prayer rose—
rays of old wounds
shone through clenched fists

hills threw down shadows of testaments—
the blue of sky stared with eye of a prophet:

and under the sun— in an instant
a shrill of birds
in unrestrained flight
tore at the heart of two histories—

Constellating
in some far Edenic place
the yearned-for light.

Chrysalis in the Desert

"... *the desert shall rejoice and blossom as the rose.*"
                                    Isaiah, 35,1.

And he says, speak to me Rachel of the time
when love healed that which was not love.
And you say, remember the chrysalis in the desert.

You write your name on the earth
history sings— high-tree in the wind

moving through time
as fire over water
as ash on ice
you listen for voice of your roots—
everywhere memory reverberates
and air— bitten into by cries
leaves its last innocence for your ears

everywhere fragments of left-behind dreams

but first your path is vivid, fibrous
through field-glow
among cypresses
to groves— humming with correspondences
between blossom, grape and grain

with your ancestor you are there
walking the meridian of morning
the scent of seven summers in your hair

there with the women of Harran
in all their othernesses
—on the same morning breath

offering libations
to a tangle of goddesses
—there clutching twig of myrtle
promise of mandrake
you alone
yearn for approval of Jacob's god
for ripeness of his myth
alone
your prayer climbs from earth toward angel
limitless with hope—

*

    So close to lightness of light
to flutterings of immortality
to music of angels and prophecy

now you are seven times blest
seven times estranged from the gods
now— across sands of centuries

seawinds brush pitted rocks of Pharos
waves testify for the future
mercantile the flow along the Nile

Greek dwells on tongues
the Law in hearts
in tenderness you dwell
sacrosanct— here with child

and quiet the stirrings of grace
quiet the joy
opening-out on Jacob's face

quiet the sun's descent
crowning trees— reclaiming paradise
but then in this world
unlocking circles of malice
hands fling stones
dislocate— eternity of a moment

your lament rings out
upward— to galaxies— to nothingness—

*And you dream of an oasis white with dew
and the glimmer of an invisible rose
growing-down from silent heaven.*

*

—A tawdry glitter of gold
a flash? illusion?

Echoes of a terrible laughter
pass across the river
—Tacitus complains about the Jews

vineyards lie harvested
Rome's streets are sultry—
autumn and hostilities grow together
—migratory birds converge
above a sunlit synagogue
wait
as you wait
for the holy letters to gather force of sorrow
for the rays to penetrate your heart

. . . cobalt as the sky
the wish to break open this strangeness

you fold into Jacob's arms
nothing other than yourself
nothing other
than being at-one-ness—

*

. . . But here are streets of doves
scented with prayer
with words of the Averroists
with leaves of the Radiant Book

streets where songs of exile
are sweet on poets' lips
where orange trees mediate between sky and dust

traders, astronomers, physicians
borrow the same currency of the earth—

rabbis carve their questions in the cloud of the Book

all the musk of Arabia and Christendom
mingles with that of the Jewry
here in streets of tolerance and flux

streets of the salamander's gaze
and the fire reflected in streets of your eyes
—Jacob journeys through them
his song sung on your breath
you name provinces of the sky

stars in your blood—
light reaches across centuries
enters the unborn
reassures the dead—

If we could measure light with our tears, you say
if we could know the altitude of our yearning
we could measure the finitude of otherness.

*

   Where summer drifts from banks of the Tagus
casting shadow— across rock
across clustering houses
tenderness grew its flower on lips—
grew in the Juderea
toward speech of paradise
then in a narrow heart
in narrow dove-coloured street
it was torn apart by anger—
behind his dead eyes
she saw all the grief of being other
she who had nurtured her love
against the will of the Talmud

when she plunged into madness
she confused a well for the wound in his soul

autumn blazed with letters of learning
as people drew tears from the well—
wept them again in the spaces between words . . .

So her legend is told, you say to Jacob.

*

 —Suddenly a butterfly the colour of earth
hovers over a thornbush
terror painted on its wings

at dawn the wound is written in the sky
at dusk a flower grows in the Book

near edge of dream
you walk through the foliage
pause at the margin of a page
turn to Jacob in the enfolding whiteness
and say— *When you speak my name*
the sound affirms my life!

    —With granite grief
you pick up your child
to crown with amen Abraham's act

all the glow of martyrdom
honeyed on your lips
withdraws into ash of silence

and they ride on, the 'errant ones'
ride on belief
hooves of their horses
crushing pasque-flowers, crocuses, grasses
—looking to stars they ride
the storehouse of hate
vanquishing stillness of forests
revelatory calls of night-birds—

their heavenblest swords transforming
even the pure into sanctified murderers

*You dream the flower questions the bud
the bud questions the seed
the seed the earth
and the earth questions God*

and God's reply is a question . . .

*

. . . Leaf-fall, memory-fall
autumn opening in your hand
—in evening's ephemeral light
the voice of history is absent
—down-reaching
branches of trees reflect in watery atoms
of a topazed world of quiet—
but the noise of time does not escape you
for the river rushes over rock
toward violence of the future
indifferent to your otherness—
you long to arrest
the towering-note of a bird
summon all words of sorrow
wing them
on a moment's equilibrium.

*

. . . Traceries burn with scrolls of the law
stucco crumbles
prayer is red with fire—
you run out clutching the seven candles
the tear in your eye, throat, mouth
with seven griefs you knock at the gate
with seven roses you wait

and the sun dies
leaves its shadow over slaughtered children
leaves no light to question God—
nights open their thighs for Jacob
he profanes in his distress—

You dream of a black lake
into which the dead leap
in the movement of water
you see an image of yourself
metamorphose
and the weight of your name
woven through history
recedes
in bright wound of new journey
—letters of the Zohar
rise up
with secrets of heaven.

*

    —And then sun over snow
and wind caressing pines
and glow of a bird folding into its wings
praise for the miracle of light—

the heartbeat of earth
tune of roots
mingling with crystal letters
there on your lips—
a hymn of Chanukah
binding you to song of the light-dwelling dead

like a dancer
across a taut wire of hope
holding high a vision and a myth
you rejoice

—traced on the sky
the yearned-for infinity of roses . . .

*

      —And in fields of sky
in fire of birds
in blossom on austere trees
throbs a potent word
it throbs
in time with devotion and usury
throbs
in howls of the city's wolves—

faith and death are the promise of spring—
cries of infidel leave fertile marks

in each Jewish heart
silence throbs
as the sun did at the edge of Massada—

with light in one hand
a rose in the other
you surrender to midnight seas
glimmering
measureless in the rabbi's tears

—vigilant
above the castle of York
an army of stars
lays bare an answer to your final fears—

Lord, let the letters of my name
resound with harmonies of the universe.

*

    . . . A figure in the wind
resolute in sanctity of twilight
you cross bridges scattered with images
turning over and over
to truth of a river
roughed-up— querulous as Job—
remembering that hour estranged from itself
that day ripening—
rowan berries flaming
like mouths ready to humiliate—
remembering alterity of colour
emptying across sky
black sun at ebb-tide—
the ship coming to halt
innocence walking leaving not one footprint
—remembering

gulls mimicking last prayer-notes
the moon casting kaddish over the water—

For every remembering, Jacob says
there is the forgetting—

For every forgetting, you reply
there is the pain of returning—
the evening sky recalls the saffron of dawn
—the night forgets the dew.

*

                      —Tongues accuse
say
autumn is stained with infants' blood
say
venom flows black from hearts of dogs
say
even waters of the moon are polluted
say
shadows across leaves bear witness
say
winter's solstice will bring grief
say
days must be salvaged from devil magic

Europe abounds with death

and the Jews' song mingles with ash of names
drifts with dust of butterflies
toward music of summer

where you imagine a swan living in tenderness
the river a cantata of joy . . .

*

—Now a house exchanged for an ass
a vineyard for bread
babble of commerce for hush of exile

across plains and mountains
you flee
clasping to heart
the pearl of your Hebrew name
in bitter almonds
an echo of it
in pomegranates
in quiet movement of sky

and all the perfumed trees of Andalusia
resonate
as if composing for you
a honeycomb of homesickness

across summer's tawny earth
fear hides in footsteps
and in the call of a solitary dove

—on thin thread-rays
nights are lit by the psalms
for stars have been diminished
by the day's lustrations
poppies of the blood blanche
grief sings like a white margarita—

You dream out of blind air
you pull roots of words
to strike a bargain with God
tendrils of silence wind about your throat—
letters lie waste in a bowl of rose dust
shadow lingers
on yesterday's utterance
of Jew
—Marrano . . .

*

—Treeless, birdless
gravity dwells in your tear

with faith in your hand
you take the silence of dusk
to light sabbath candles

snow— light as a promise
falls indifferently

a tailor speaks with a peddler
a merchant with an elder
salutations wing in the direction of stars

in Lublin, Warsaw, Frankfurt
Venice or Vilnius?
It doesn't matter which
for in each place
flowers the same image
and in each soul
one rose
nourished by the one nostalgia—

and when
carrying voice of an angel
the east wind penetrates night's yearning
the oil lamp flickers—
you watch the space between wick and shadow
bread and piety gladden the table
fruit has the skin of autumn
flesh of thanksgiving—
a bowl of petalled water ripples—

in the silence
you are a guest on earth like any other
then words and silence are blown together.

*

   —Written on the heart
joy of the rose
Purim-joy— deliverance—
murmurings of the day
tune to far away laughter through juniper trees
somewhere a prince
calls out to a Jew with gentleness
your voice caresses Jacob—
a raven dips its wings
in the noon reflection of the sun
longing and hope turn on the one axis
. . . then in a ditch
the remains of a woman
a Cossack riding over her
—the scream
pierces the ear of the universe.

And this woman
rushing through history
stops to take breath in the cold light

—the dead weave their names into hers
—moss grows on branches of prayer.

*

      —Threaded light
grown into lore and legend
an exchange between past and future
—you are in streets
nerved with poverty and music
with festive Seder hands
offering remembrance to children

in streets of intimacy and hope

Jacob takes your leafage of love
mirrors the fruit of it—
you speak in a language
nocturnal, crystal
yearn for the golden rose
you imagine blooming
on the cosmic mountain of Jerusalem
but midnight surprises
stuttering in Edenic embrace—

You dream you run through gates of the ghetto
to where the moon
hangs over an immense space
like an amulet—

pines smell of regeneration
quietly the river flows
taking crisp leaves of memory with it

letters of otherness dissolve in the light

all the wisdom of womanhood
you bring to your argument with God.

*

  Voices of forests shelter voices of fugitives
rivers speak of death
stone of the dilemma of Kahals

(Jew condemned to be hunter of Jew?)

with only the taste of faith on their lips
the pious petition God on parchment of dawn
—yesterday's lamentation is rewritten
—Israel's myth quivers

... each night when your limbs rest against Jacob's
you say, *God needs our questions—*
each night he takes a candle from his heart
and says
This is the stubborn flame of our people
this has no question ...

  —Questionless, weightless
wrapped in prayer of the Baal Shem-Tov
you dream you climb to the peak of a mountain—
the white of consonants sings

red and green exchange their infinity
the blue of summer
abandons its fruits of anguish
below you
the lake into which you will fall
ripples with the enigmas of night
as if reflecting a covenant with nothing—

and you push
against the gates of imagination
shutting an eye
on the hoarfrost and future—

*

—On a beacon of time the lindens
reaching to coral skies
as if they were covenants for tomorrows

—Berlin summers
textures of silk, ambition, throats of women
are washed by the evening sun—
self-hatred flutters
like a moth with bronze wings

Yiddish is swept to corners of rooms
words of Goethe galvanise tongues
ironies of the soul are exposed
in the wit of young Heine—
dream, promise and self-thinking are confused

—at what edge of your vision
do the shadows of history
confront you in the eyes of another?

for there from the ghetto the rose of shame
there the angel of remembrance
there the humiliation and arrogance
there the image of the Jew

*—there from the image
comes our madness and wisdom,* Jacob says

—there from your tear
comes the laughter, self-mocking, nostalgic—

It is not us they hate, you say
it is the image of our madness in their souls.

*

   —And your soul returns for solace
to a land once sweet-haven—
stones disclose memories of stars
air crowds
with syllables of Yiddish
the dead
reclaim dignity of name
ceremony of commerce
a tremor of the south
in a cantor's voice
ornaments guttural threads of faith
morning gathers-in nostalgia

. . . you walk streets of light
hearing history trade in darknesses

with tempo of a slow intermezzo
the Vistula flows under the willows—
leaves yellow with a language of hope
tossed them by finches
the texture of the hour is luminous—

*Like the bloom of a January rose
in the garden shared by Jew and Pole*
you say—

Like memory before it ebbs beyond reach
Jacob replies.

*

—Throwing about your shoulder
a thin shawl of laughter
you turn in the half light
to protect yourself from coming winds
dusk fills your ears
with song of a bird whose wings are broken—

you raise a fist
but letters want to flow from your fingertips
inscribe your name
where the silence of the moon
acknowledges all crime against all otherness

—through tall trees
light conducts its message
to the ear of all hearing ones

—between one world and another
jug in hand
an angel waits for the tears . . .

*

      Grating of arpeggios—
echoes of the east
in throats of returning swallows

and caravans of cloud
scurrying where? you ask—

in the garden you have made with love
a bee desires the rose unable to open
a drop of rain lingers on an autumn leaf
the oak tree lullabies the ash

vibrant with myth
a ram's horn fades into nothing of aether
before the holy ark strewn petals wither
a dark pulse travels over the Danube
a black waltz begins—
our waltz, you say . . .

under unaware stars
in fractured time— you waltz
on breath of history hammered by rhetoric

waltz through streets emptying of Jews
waltz along a vertical line
descending
to the night
of crystal

no place now for fear to hide
only the game of seek, seek . . .

*

—Again and again
this dream of Eve beside you
holding a mirror to the world

Beloved daughter, Eve says
come with me to the meadows of ash
come, gather the names of the murdered
come, for each letter there is a prayer
for the snow-white raven
the one which will fly from the summit of pain
on a future intelligence of light

against speech of ice-winds
you enter an immeasurable landscape
night becomes day
day becomes the hands of years
recollecting the dead
and their silence sings-out
to a sacred metronome of the earth—
sings with the voices of rivers
with sands of disputed shores
with leaves changing colour
in birch forests of the east—
sings with the high-key of pines
with the murmur of undergrowth

with all the cries of disregarded angels.

*

—You hear your name in the air
on breath through a Levantine flute
hear it in glitter of water
through field-glow
among cypresses—
in a blade of grass
you hear echoes
of promise and betrayal
in a stone
catastrophe
in a collision of myths

and the sun
sharpens the dust of poverty
glares over gestures of those dispossessed

—and you dream
of the bird coming out of exile
carrying in its mouth
syllables of justice
—dream
you cross carnelian sands
stumble through mirages
stammering your way
to where wounds cry out
in towns and villages—
in cherished olive groves—
in valleys
where citrus is the colour
worn down by despair
and the blossoming of jasmine
a time of violence
—dream

of history speaking-out
as if each instant
were jailer of the past
—dream of Hagar's lament
of the breaking-off of branches
for leaves of the future
—dream
of the chrysalis in the desert
and the butterfly
journeying through the world
on the scent of roses
—dream
of an upsurge of prayer

'Let the persecuted not be the persecutors'

In my otherness, O Lord.

*

  —And so in the violet hour you walk
piecing together fragments of narrative
here, beside another voice of another river

starlings have left shadows
and their shrill notes of chatter
still echo on the wind with tumult of the day

with all that is written in memory and dream

tuned to the turning world
your name summers—

but as each moment passes
time offers no promise
and you hear
even in the grasping of ivy
a fierce cry for roots—

to the enigma of water
you commit your fealty
look for the image cast in your name
—find how you are bound
to a fable of being
to a dance of the divine
shining— here
with frailty of the chrysalis . . .

*Speak to me, Jacob, of the time
when love healed that which was not love . . .*

Here Over the Midnight Sea

Here over the midnight sea— a miracle of stars
radiant, prayerlike, untangling
an inheritance of fear
imbibed by clustering, cliff-grasping, trees

here an octave of quiet
in which a solitary gull carries the salt of wisdom
as if it were in full-throat of exile

here the covenant between air and ear
a begetter of promises—
the moon's pull on waves
a lullaby to hush the violated—
the pulse of history
a lilt through the indifferent universe

here all that is palpable retunes to mythic spheres
and the dead haunt the souls of the living

here, until time itself annuls.

Light-Speech

               (Cézanne)

There on the retina— light-speech of sky
trees, sun-soaked Provençal earth
there a priesthood of colour
violating a moment:
only slowly does the image
let go what is nerve-torn—
only slowly does harmony
reach the hand waiting with brush—
only slowly mingles
breath of nature, prayer and art.

               (Van Gogh)

—Yes, your eye upturned the blue
from that pulsing loneliness
but it was your soul
anticipating its beloved sun's eclipse
which winnowed the field and transformed the yellow.
With the ray of death you painted the crows.

(Redon)

Ophelia among the flowers
the light of her dead self penetrating the moon
—lamp for all spurned lovers.

(Constable)

Virgilian painter
with what fugal force
did you mark the metamorphosing cumulus?
Amid what chatter of birds
did time become in your hand
the eternity of colour?
What bee hummed close to your ear
when the morning lifted
and the sun
raked the liturgy of the fields?
So—the hedgerows of East Bergholt
have diminished—
no longer the breath of moral will
nor the undulations of heart
can be heard— here
where you learnt to catch
the exchange of light between presence and absence.

(Morandi)

And these jugs, jars, vases
orphans of light
isolated in their silences
tenderly you place
as if between the movements
of a favourite string quartet—
your eye attending colour and form
as it would your loved one's flesh.
Then begins the translation
of *natura morta*
into essences in dialogue with life.

(Goya)

But there was that error
of light
etched line by line—
that black irony
that shiver of air
and estranged honeyed sky
over the wasteland of Zaragoza—
that climb into cruelty
to chimes of a bell
ringing out the terror of war
minute by minute—
that unredeemed cry
that passes through centuries.

(Masaccio's Exiled Eve)

How was it in the Garden
when all the colours dazzled your eyes?

How was it beneath the Tree
when leafage reflected
rootward and heavenward in rivers of joy?

How did the light fall on snowdrop and crocus
in such purity of air?

How was it to walk in company of an angel
innocent of crepuscular words
brooding, womblike, on the winds?

How was it when yes and no were fearless—
when winged on God's language
dove and hawk
crowned with amen music of the spheres?

How was it before the sun of Babel—
before burgeoning betrayal
before auras of lies?

How was it before stone and sky
witnessed the first murder—
before script of grasses
bore testimony for the future?

How was it, then, before day and night
gathered crystalline tears
shed by history's angel—

before rays of your grief
became the first lamp of yearning?

(Piero Della Francesca)

In an instant was it there
all that rounded sadness
in the saint's magnetic eyes?
Into their vast quiet we enter
—into remembrance
of the world's wounded soul.
On arc of grace
time moves forward and backward
as if the moon were telling
of visitation of an angel.
All in-dwelling— all light-speech
here reverberates at one with revelation.

Gorse-Light

Gorse-light
cradling fire of Languedoc earth
from which I grow
toward some kind of tranquillity.

The lark ascends its song.
History's wounds retreat
hide in wide promise of sky.

As if it were a book of Cathar or Kabbalist
I open the quiet . . .

—Undoing the silence
chatter of an unknown bird
monotonous call of a cicada
a butterfly addressing the grass
then fall of shadow over muttering hills
and scent of wind-awry petals
undoing the past . . .

The woman looks within
to the girl she has betrayed—

Amid mallow and celandine
a scattering of her dreams in near-distant field.

Hawkweed and poppy in the wind
and the gulls
like emissaries, you say
bringing the gift
of an intense silver sky
just as they did
when the air was thick with omens
and the fields
planted according to Pliny
smelt of infinity and the presence of gods.

—And when the hour surrenders
to quiet of the garden
purple-tongued irises
speak to blades of listening grasses

like a magician
an emerald-eyed lizard emerges
darts along the stone wall
rediscovering Spring—

light crowns funereal cypresses
falls on foliage of young vines
salvages fragments of myth—

on ray of memory— a crow
once all-whiteness
once all-dazzling obeisance
caws as if in protest to a god.

In plenitude of being
we offer-up our silence to the sun.

But to speak, o earth, of your vineyards
and your vigilant pines
as if they could bring forth the past—
or to ask remembrance of asphodel and poppy?

—then to draw near
to the hushed hymn of your mountains
those ever-pure witnesses.

The lilt of winter haunting blossoms
is charged with contraries
and the sun leaves shadow over a goldfinch's longing.

I seek the moment
the fleeting might-have-been moment
before the birth of a troubadour's song
before the whisperings of Elijah in ears of attentive rabbis.

I seek in the name of the long ago massacred
my breath drawn from Languedoc's scars.

Knowing-Well of Silence

> *"TO STAND in the shadow*
> *of the scar up in the air".*
> Paul Celan

Nowhere the last vibration of the last violin
nowhere the last cry of an angel
only brick struck dumb
and sky coloured autumn
as if by revenants of the children

nowhere the high-song of a bird
its breath drawn from cold air of history
just a magpie disturbing earth
covering the murdered
just a tremor through grasses
and the sun in its place
—oblivious:

your heart gestures toward mine
from the knowing-well of silence
—the nowhere of atonement
for those whom you can never atone for.

But irony makes its way to the heart
here where violins obeyed the hand
of the megalo-dreaming maestro
and myth flowered marguerite-bright
beneath vibratile skies

now as starlings— gathering-in
brush the stone ears of saints with chatter
the evening prelude is of a different kind—

We walk the path beside the Elbe
talk fervently between shadows
of this and that— of othernesses
our voices pitched
so that the dead may hear our questions
—raked through an undergrowth of years.

We take tea and speak of the dead
—the Jews' dead, Dresden's dead
you on one side of the table
myself on the other
night unfolding in fading twitter of birds:

our light sought in words
pursuing God and His nothingness.

—Then at dusk voices of the dead
reach us through the leaves—
we grasp them like shadows
to be transcribed
on a white field of paper—

the movement of the pen
witnessed by stars
witnessing indescribable light.

And everywhere voices of the dead
the loved and the unloved—
mingling with leaves
with wisdom in the throats of birds

mingling with Job's cry
still heard on the wind
with autumn's hubbub on the river

the hush of angels
mingling with remembrance
with singing dust—
the knowing yes
mingling with the knowing no

and earth turns
retuning to the narrative
and under the scar
— crystal-clear
we listen.

She Sings This Perfect City

She sings this perfect city—
I wander her streets
like some kind of novice
seeking an instrument
upon which to accompany her.
Doming intimacies
between God-reaching music and spires
September's sky broods.

—But imagine
throbbing through the air
Yitzkor—
an ascent of letters
remembering the One unnameable
and the many
thousand pronounceable names

then imagine an axe at noon
the sun absorbing death
without the dying

the light chronicled here
on Prague's sorrowful walls.

Roman Hour

This hour amid the hush of candles
vibratile Roman hour—
hour creeping down time
toward sanctuary of another
he, the first lord of light, warrior of stars.

This hour we stammer our way into
hour of the hart, dove, vine-tendril
emblems for the dead man in his coffin.

Hour of otherness in which we ask
do we trespass with our senses?

This hour we breathe one language of grief.

Lord of this hour
let the dead be nurtured—
let them from emptiness blossom.

And even the sea-seeking pines
voice confidence of being
here in a leavened smile of the city

taking breath
where columns of laughter
passed from ancient to baroque
light-bearing branches
broker between sky and earth

where stone speaks to stone
of autumn in the hands of Caesars
they speak to the sun
of resurrection and gods—

in the image of themselves they stand
scenting the air
as if to console future with past
for shadow rises in the sap
grows from the throat of Rome
upward
to near-edge of hubris.

. . . Remembrance, he wrote
would be of exquisite waters
steps like waves, nights, gardens.

Did he not hear at breaking of dawn
nature's prayer
for the ears of Rome's dead—

nor the musk-toned dusk
in which the butterflies dance
their fluttering arabesques
and the bronze smile of the boy
offers his innocence
to Ceres, Diana and Aphrodite forever?

But now how the river rushes on
throwing off remembrance
of the watery-eyed ghetto—

the plane trees offer their silence.

I imagine cool reflections of women
laundering rhetoric of myth
with the mysteries of their otherness—
those wearing the vanities of Rome
those in their drab Jewish dress.

But how the river rushes on
throwing off remembrance
of the holy candelabrum
and Titus' love for Berenice.

Faustina

> *"Godlike, the man who*
> *sits at her side, who*
> *watches and catches*
> *that laughter."*
> Catullus

And then like a surprised bird
laughter rose from your throat
—all glitter of pearls
woven through hair
scented with sandalwood
all modesty
fell to the flesh of night.
Etched you were
in the heart of the Emperor
grave, virtuous—
but with fire in his absence
you rode erotic hymns
celebrating the love-goddess
—and when
confronting your sister-self
in that joy-dance
blue and pure, there
in the young pantomimus' eye
the bird broke loose
winging— shameless, light toward light.

Toward the Midnight

"*This Journey to Italy wakes me at daylight every morning
and haunts me horribly*".
                Keats' letter to John Taylor, 13 August 1820

. . . And when dawn ministered
and the scent of Roman earth
cradled the coffin
February smiled the smile irony forgot—

(ah, did the simple grave-digger know?)

for the breath that came like ice
had hardened the letters of your name
already writ in a flux of water
and time would not let go
light held so long in a hand—

nor would the songbird relent
nor the violet lose remembrance.

—Exiled, yet near she was
your death her falling
into days of brokenness

the crocuses' thrust
the exchange between sparrow and star
illumined her loss

it was the pulse of each letter
sprung from your blood
that nurtured—

light through which she moved
utterly possessed
inhaling tendernesses and doubts
as if they, only they, could keep her alive
there in the memory
of that immeasurable country
where to be
was to be once blest.

Rich the heartland of poppies
from which her words rose
that summer-full day:
uncertainties of your universe
had intensified passion
and those shining moments
you imbibed— fragile as the flowers.

Each night she knew
how the moon had thrown light
on your all-seeking soul-identity—

knew how the dark voice of the sea
had cajoled anxiety:

how each utterance
rising
in imagination's monastery

was fire of heart
singing you
to the land of the dead—

Long in her grief
she walked through the tangle
of bracken and leaves—
heard in the tremor
and in the sky
charged lilac with remembrance
a canon of beauty and truth—
stored it in her being
as you did
toward the midnight of salvation.

Over and over— she plunged
words of your death
in memory—

her hands gathering leaves of thought
her ashened-lips
moving in and out of midnight's language

each poem
a radiance reflected
in the wells of her eyes.

He wept, the young Jew, with jealousy
when there he stumbled into them.

Yesterday's Domain

Spiritus-rose, the one I smell in my dreams
the one with the golden corolla
ever-blooming, ever-remembering, Eros now silent.

Scenting the hour— a crepuscular rose
in yesterday's domain

I leap into the eye of nostalgia
you hesitate between desire and guilt
—time divides us

then you speak of music as if it were love
the silence from which it comes
enigma to which it reaches
and a simple thread draws us
to the place where blind tenderness belongs.

My unshed tear you recognise.

But here, guiltless, with me you climb
a stony path up the mountain—

This is where truth about you and I
meets the purity of sky, I hear you say.

The peak is shrouded—
soon summer rain
will wash away— remembrance.

. . . Now we lift a lamp over the past
disturb those rowan-berry days
when autumn lulled us on fragile loyalty.

A swallow flies south on sharp-edge of memory
and you do not see as I do.

Dark-eyed, I confront your blue
the swimming-in blue
where joy died— and birthed again and again.

—And so we, like the angels
require a turning of breath to unravel our past
the long ago play— marriage of essences.

But when— as if with thud of a coin
(once tossed by love)
anger quickens
all that was unhealable endures, glows.

Thief to myself I bury the smile of a god.
You bury irony in the quiet of earth.

Crystal-fall, one by one, blown by the wind
memory snowed-over—

the rose of yesterday's domain
considers its future.

Waiting for foliage
to unfurl a draft of early April promise
birds deliver fertile song through trees.

We leaf together fragments of the past.

Memory what shall I do with you?
You who like a fox expose conspiracy
between snow and the moon's light
here where I have forbidden trespass—

what shall I do with the uninhabitable
unburiable, shards—
with recollection of the I wishing to be not?

—yet come a clearing in the sky
come sun-threads
I can turn from the image of the I that was

in lower strata of heart
there is seed of self-forgiveness—

And what was the homeland I imagined
when we spoke of journeying
to once upon a time?

Does yesterday's rose yearn for its bud
or the pebble for rock?

Does dust hold to memory as if it were pure light?

An eye sees what it wants to see
the mind jokes
invents angels of necessity
whose messages we believe are love.

I tell you— nostalgia is a dance
a waltz around a mulberry bush
in all seasons—

we falter there— between one truth and another.

Fragments

1

And in the whiteness of an interregnum
the shout of poppies is violent—
We move in a field of dream
through the uncertainties of summer.
The sky taunts us with eternity.

2

Honey-glow— falling
over February's bare branches
one blackbird, one song.
In our room— emptying
of evening's last images
Schnabel's impassioned Beethoven
also reaches toward unknowable godhead.

3

Against speech of the wind
against rain on our lips
we tread through last year's leaves
—in their silence
they haunt us with desires.

4

And from the tree of death
leaves of our lives
deep-veined with memory—
love running through ripe as autumn.

5

Who said age was a lonely shore
and memory like a shell held to the ear?
Who said the sky leaves the sea
when dusk wrestles with night?

6

Primrose-night— full of promise
taking the soul from emptiness
to glow of vision
there on the wing of a migrating bird.
The eye of the insomniac moon
reflects the transient blessing.

7

Anxiety—
an axe breaking open dawn
each particle of light
re-entering darkness—
In each darkness
a clenched fist
longs for the sun at noon.

8

Haunt me, o flute
like the first reed
played by an Egyptian boy
brought rays of the sun
to quieten a river:
haunt me with a tune
rooted in the sky
when I fall from grace
into anger . . .

9

The wind about us
the sea all-animal— all-grey.
With one hand

I hold the weight of the hour
with the other— eternity's map.
I take the air as I would an offering
from near-drowning.

10

Lullabying the sky
through an open window
drift of a Schubert andante.
Lullabying the sea
memories, dense as these pebbles
vibrating in my hand—
fragments
on an empty, nocturnal, beach.

NOTES:

Rivers and Revenants

Page 10: *Vytautas*, Grand Duke of Lithuania, had encouraged migrating Jews to settle in Lithuania and had granted them a special charter of protection in 1388. Lithuania was still pagan at this time and therefore more tolerant of the Jews.

— *Žemyna*, Lithuanian goddess of the earth and fertility.

— *Chazan* is Hebrew for cantor.

Page 11: The *Dabikiné* is a small river in rural north west Lithuania, which was part of the Russian Pale of Settlement.

— *Kiddush*, a prayer in celebration of the Sabbath.

— *The May Laws* were severe restrictive measures taken against the Jews in 1882 by the Russian government. Alexander II had been assassinated the previous year and the revolutionaries had called on the people to rebel. To protect itself the regime had found the usual scapegoat, hence mass waves of emigration.

Page 12: *'grief-flow of the murdered'* alludes to 1941–42.

Page 13: There are many legends about Elijah on all levels of Jewish religious consciousness, from that of the mystic to the Jew who saw him simply as a friend sent from God in times of distress.

— *Avaslan* is the name of the family farmstead. It was burnt down by hostile peasants after it had been vacated by the family.

— The stork is Lithuania's national bird; it nests in nearly every farm.

Page 15: The crow in Lithuanian folklore is the bearer of spirits from the other side.

— *'Word— our word'* is Israel.

Crowned by Death

Page 36: *Cassiel*, the angel of solitudes and tears.

How Distant You Were

Page 39: *Kaddish*, prayer recited in memory of a relative, usually a parent.

Chrysalis in the Desert

Page 42: *'So close to lightness of light'*: this passage alludes to the flourishing diaspora in Alexandria, until Jew-baiting became an issue from about 40AD.

Page 44: *Averroists*: Averroes (1126–1189), the foremost Aristotelian in Spain who influenced Jewish philosophy.

— *The Radiant Book,* the Zohar of the Kabbalists, compiled in the 13thC by Moses de Leon.

Page 45: The legend is that of Rachel of Toledo, who lost her reason when her father stabbed to death the Christian with whom she was in love. The street became known as that of the Bitter Well.

Page 46: The *'errant ones'* were the Crusaders, as described by Solomon bar Simson (1453) when chronicling the fate of the Jews in central Europe during the first Crusade: many slaughtered themselves and their children rather than convert to Christianity.

Page 48: '. . . *Traceries burn with scrolls of the law'*: Victims of the Castilian monarchy, a great number of Jews of Toledo and Andalusia were massacred and their synagogues burnt in the summer of 1391.

Page 49/50: Waves of anti-Judaic feeling invaded England at the time of the third Crusade. In March 1190, the Jews of York sought refuge in the castle to avoid massacre, but it became evident there was to be no deliverance and the rabbi led them to mass suicide. This had occurred at Massada in 70 AD, when the Romans had besieged the fortress in which the Jews had been holding out.

Page 50/51: *'remembering the hour estranged from itself'*: Edward I of England prohibited the practice of usury and attempted to divert the Jews into agriculture. The experiment failed, and on July 18th 1290, a decree was issued ordering all Jews to leave the country. A large ship carrying many wealthy Jews was deliberately grounded on a sandbank at the mouth of the Thames, the passengers were invited to disembark and then abandoned. They drowned when the tide rose; their property was divided between the sailors.

Page 51: The Jews were blamed by the clerics for the Black Death of 1348/49. They were accused of poisoning the rivers and wells with the intent to kill Christians, also of ritual infanticide.

Page 52: *'Now a house exchanged for an ass'* refers to the expulsion of the Jews from Spain in 1492.

Page 53: *Marrano*, pig, the derogatory term used against the Spanish Jews forced to convert to Christianity; most, however, retaining a secret adherence to Judaism.

Page 54: 'The remains of a woman': In 1648, the Cossacks of the Ukraine, under their helmsman Chmielnicki, rose against their oppression by the Poles and massacred the Jews because so many of them worked for the Poles.

Page 55: *Seder* is the ritual meal on the first night of the Passover.

Page 56: *Kahals* were the Jewish Councils, and responsible for supplying the Jewish conscription into the Russian Army (by edict of Nicholas I in 1827 to replace the Jewish tax). If they failed to supply the necessary quota they were obliged to offer themselves.

— *Baal Shem Tov* (1700–60), mystic and first leader of the Hasidic movement.

Page 57: '... *self thinking*', a term used by Lessing (1729–81), the German poet and philosopher.

Page 58: '*sweet-haven*' was Poland. The Hebrew *Polin* is rooted in the words *po lin*, meaning there find rest or haven.

Page 59: '... *the garden shared by Jew and Pole*' alludes to January 1863 when many of Warsaw's Jews joined with the Poles in rising against Russia's annexation.

Page 60: '*an angel waits for the tears*': according to Hasidic legend there is an angel who collects tears in a huge jug, when the jug is filled to the brim it will be a sign of the end of human suffering.

— The ram's horn (shofar) is blown ritually in the synagogue, especially at the close of the Day of Atonement.

— '*to the night/of crystal*': Kristallnacht, November 1938, when Nazi party members smashed and looted Jewish shops, burnt down synagogues and made random arrests.

Page 63: '*Let the persecuted not be the persecutors*' is from the title of a poem by the German/Jewish poet, Nelly Sachs.

Light-Speech

Page 68: Goya's *The Disasters of War* came first from a commission to go to Zaragoza and record the effect of the Napoleonic army's siege there.

Page 70: Piero della Francesca: the poem is a meditation on the fragment, St. Julian.

Gorse-Light

Page 72: The all-white crow was a messenger for the gods; when failing to deliver a message for Apollo on time was then punished by having its feathers turned black.

Knowing-Well of Silence
Page 74: The poem refers to a visit to Terezin in the company of a German friend.
— *'here where violins obeyed the hand'* refers to the Opera House at Dresden; the hand is Wagner's.

She Sings This Perfect City
Page 77: The city is Prague, the *'sorrowful walls'* are those of the memorial to the 70,000 Bohemian and Moravian victims of the Holocaust, their names scripted on walls of the Pinkus Synagogue in the old Jewish quarter.
— *Yitzkor,* a Jewish memorial prayer for the dead, particularly for relatives.

Roman Hour
Page 78: *'This hour amid the hush of candles'* relates to the 12th century church of San Clemente, built on the foundations of an early 4th century church, and that built over a Mithraic Temple.
Page 79: *'Remembrance, he wrote . . .'* Rilke's letter to Lou Andreas-Salomé, 3rd November, 1903.
Page 80: Rome's Jewish ghetto was frequently flooded by the Tiber. Drabness of dress was in moral opposition to the Christians, whose lavish clothes the Jews considered to be an evil to be avoided.

Faustina
Page 81: History is not quite certain of Faustina's character, Marcus Aurelius praised her as a perfect wife in his Meditations, but other sources claimed she was far from virtuous; among her known lovers was a pantomimus (a Roman dancer).

Toward the Midnight
Page 82/85: *'the breath that came like ice'* was Joseph Severn's as he leant over the dying man. Keats wished to be remembered by "Here lies one whose name was writ in water", later engraved on his tombstone. Violets and daises grew over the tomb, the

violets picked by his admirers for remembrance.
— Keats had forbidden Fanny Brawne to accompany him to Italy because he didn't want her to see him dying.
— In a letter to Fanny from the Isle of Wight, July 1819, Keats had asked her to write to him with words as rich as a draught of poppies.
— When Fanny heard of Keats' death she shut herself in her room, read and reread his letters to her. She went for long walks on her own over Hampstead Heath, where they had often walked together, staying out so late at night someone would have to come and find her to bring her home. Many years later, Fanny married a young Sephardic Jew.

www.ingramcontent.com/pod-product-compliance
Lightning Source LLC
Chambersburg PA
CBHW031159160426
43193CB00008B/444